THE HAYLING ISLAND BRANCH

(THE HAYLING BILLY)

THE HAYLING ISLAND BRANCH

(THE HAYLING BILLY)

John Scott-Morgan

PEN & SWORD
TRANSPORT

AN IMPRINT OF PEN & SWORD BOOKS LTD.
YORKSHIRE – PHILADELPHIA

First published in Great Britain in 2019 by
Pen and Sword Transport
An imprint of
Pen & Sword Books Ltd
Yorkshire - Philadelphia

ISBN 978 1 52672 681 0

A CIP catalogue record for this book is available from the British Library.

Typeset by Aura Technology and Software Services, India
Printed and bound in India by Replika Press Pvt. Ltd.

Pen & Sword Books Ltd incorporates the Imprints of Pen & Sword Books Archaeology,
Atlas, Aviation, Battleground, Discovery, Family History, History, Maritime, Military,
Naval, Politics, Railways, Select, Transport, True Crime, Fiction, Frontline Books, Leo
Cooper, Praetorian Press, Seaforth Publishing, Wharncliffe and White Owl.

For a complete list of Pen & Sword titles please contact

PEN & SWORD BOOKS LIMITED
47 Church Street, Barnsley, South Yorkshire, S70 2AS, England
E-mail: enquiries@pen-and-sword.co.uk
Website: www.pen-and-sword.co.uk

or

PEN AND SWORD BOOKS
1950 Lawrence Rd, Havertown, PA 19083, USA
E-mail: Uspen-and-sword@casematepublishers.com
Website: www.penandswordbooks.com

Contents

Introduction

The Hayling Island branch was one of Britain's most enchanting railways, originally promoted and constructed by a local private company. The first section of the line was opened to freight, from Havant to Langston harbour, in January 1865. A further extension of the line, over a timber viaduct to its terminus at the south end of the island, opened on 28 June 1867, with public services operating from 16 July.

The railway was at first operated by the local company, on a sub contacted basis, with the contractor Frederick Furniss providing the motive power and carriage stock. The local company operated the branch for the first eight years, after which, from January 1872, the London Brighton & South Coast Railway operated the railway on behalf of the local company, (LB&SCR). On 1 January 1923, the Southern Railway took over the line and the local company ceased to exist; the branch in turn became part of British Railways Southern Region at Nationalisation on 1 January 1948.

The Hayling Island branch finally closed to all traffic, on Saturday, 2 November 1963, when Terrier tank 32650, heading a six carriage train, with Terrier 32662 assisting at the rear, left the terminus at Hayling Island for the last time with a public train service at 9 in the evening. On the following day, a farewell special headed by the oldest Terriers, 32636 and 32670, was operated along the line by the Locomotive Club of Great Britain.

An attempt was made to reopen the line using a single deck former Blackpool tram, but to no avail, as the line was eventually lifted and demolished, a few years after closure.

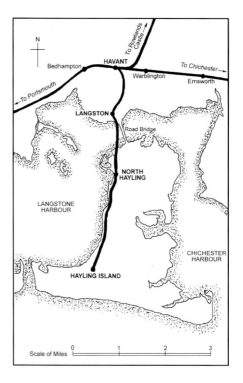

The Line's History

The coastline from Brighton to Portsmouth, with its coastal towns, villages and inlets, was once an important aspect of trade and commerce, in the South of England. Despite the importance of trade along this coast, there was a certain remoteness about the area; Hayling Island was one of the districts that suffered from poor connections with other parts of the surrounding area.

It was not until 1822 that a road bridge was constructed to connect the mainland with the island, this being financed by the Duke of Norfolk, whose family had manorial rights at that time. The need for improved public transport did not change until 1847, with the opening of the London Brighton & South Coast Railway's main line from Chichester to Portsmouth.

The LB&SCR opened a station at Havant, which much improved transport links in the area making it possible to travel to London within hours, instead of having to undergo a long and often uncomfortable coach journey.

The local people wanted to improve transport in the district and the first steps to this were the promotion of a tramway company to connect Havant with the bridge that linked the island to the mainland. This was authorised in the Hayling Bridge & Causeway Act of 1851. The Act allowed the company to purchase the road bridge from a Mr Padwick, who had acquired the manorial rights from the Duke of Norfolk by that time. The construction of the tramway never took place and the parliamentary powers were allowed to lapse.

In 1858, the second main line arrived in Havant, in the form of the Portsmouth Direct line. This was a private speculative venture by contractor Thomas Brassey, who, after constructing the formation from Godalming to Havant, offered the line to anyone who wished to purchase it. A Dutch auction between the London & South Western Railway, (L&SWR), and the South Eastern Railway then occurred as a result of Thomas Brassey's policy, resulting in the railway being leased and later purchased by the London & South Western Railway company. However, before this took place, a serious dispute between the L&SWR and the LB&SCR took place, culminating in the battle of Havant, when on 1 January 1859, the L&SWR tried to run a freight train across the junction linking the Portsmouth direct line with the LB&SCR main line from Chichester to Portsmouth.

The result was a fight at Havant station between a group of navvies from the L&SWR and another group of navvies from the LB&SCR, trying to prevent the freight train running through. After arbitration, it was decided by a judge that the L&SWR should have running powers across the junction and access to the LB&SCR main line to Portsmouth, which from then on should be operated as a joint line.

The local population observed the legal wrangling between the two main line companies with great interest and soon realised that the two large companies had little interest in their needs or wishes. The result of this was the setting up of a new local railway company, to construct a line across the island.

The Hayling Railway Company was formed, which by Act of Parliament of 23 July 1860 was authorised to run a line from Havant, following the natural course, for two miles curving south to Langston, where the formation would cross a substantial timber viaduct, with a swing bridge to allow sea-going craft to use Langston harbour. The formation would then continue along the island's western coast line, running out to sea on an embankment to a terminus at Sinah Point, on the south-west tip. It was hoped to reclaim 1,000 acres of land from the sea along this part of the coast, to the benefit of the local population.

It took a considerable amount of time to appoint a board of directors and raise the £50,000 needed to start the construction of the line. Like so many local railways of this period, even with the best intensions, only £38,565 was ever raised locally, resulting in £11,000 having to be found in loans and debenture stock by the company. It was not until the spring of 1863 that contracts were awarded and construction actually began on the formation of the railway. The engineers appointed for the project were Messrs Hayter and Jay, the contractor being Frederick Furniss.

Despite exaggerated prices being demanded by local land owners, on the Havant to Langston section the contractor managed to make steady progress until by August 1864, the engineers could report that the line as far as Langston Key was completed and ready for freight traffic. There were also short sections of line completed further south at this time; the engineers reporting that, they intended to start construction of a section of line from Sinah Point, at the far end of the railway, and it was hoped that the completed line would be able to open to traffic, late in the following summer. The directors felt jubilant at this report and proposed the construction of a further extension of one and a quarter miles along the south beach from Sinah Point, to South Hayling, with a view to constructing a small port. The company managed to obtain an Act of Parliament for this purpose, passed on 14 July 1864, which allowed the company to raise the extra capital to carry out these additional works.

Although the first section of the railway opened to freight traffic in January 1865, from Havant to Langston Key, work on the rest of the line slowed and then stopped altogether as a result of problems with constructing the embankment along the west coast of the island, the contractor reporting that the cost of construction on this section of the line was costing more than the revenue derived from the newly opened section, from Havant to Langston Key, which was making only £10 a mile per week.

The construction sites along the length of the line were left abandoned and in isolation at this time, with a partially completed timber viaduct at the north end and two sections of completed embankment along the west coast near Sinah Point being all there was to show for all the hard toil of those engaged in the line's construction. Over a year was to go by before any movement in the line's fortunes could be observed, during which interest seemed to dwindle, both locally and with those who had invested in the project.

Shareholders' meetings were called in 1866 and 1867; however, as a result of few people turning up to the meetings, a quorum could not be formed and in both years, the meetings were adjourned. In 1868, enough people did turn up to allow a proper meeting and those who attended were surprised to hear how much progress had taken place, despite the difficulties that had beset the company. Those attending the meeting learned that Mr Padwick, successor to the Duke of Norfolk as Lord of the Manor, had died and Mr Frances Fuller, a land agent from London, had purchased considerable stretches of land on the island.

Fuller was a very enterprising man, who had plans for the island and developing the land he had purchased. He knew that the island had great potential as a resort, where people could spend their leisure time and holiday. Hayling Island was in easy distance from London, with good train services provided by both the L&SWR and the LB&SCR, via Havant; all the island needed was a good railway connection and some serious investment. Fuller also quickly understood that the company had made a major blunder by trying to construct a railway over mud flats along the western coast, with the result of ongoing extra cost. Quite sensibly, he was convinced the only way to get this railway constructed was to build it on solid dry land. He had the line resurveyed along the western shore, purchased the land needed and instructed the contractor to start work, after joining the board of directors. A bill was put through Parliament, which received royal assent on 12 August 1867, to allow the new works to begin.

Faced with a new enthusiasm and the right sort of organising spirit, the contractor very quickly constructed the three miles of track needed to complete the island railway and also finished the timber viaduct. Such was the progress under its new management that the company was able to open the line for through passenger traffic on 28 June 1867, with a public service commencing on 16 July, of that year. The railway's passenger service was withdrawn during the winter of 1867-8 but reinstated permanently in the New Year.

Fuller was not letting the grass grow under his feet, during this period, as he was involved with setting up a golf course and a horse racing course. The shareholders who attended the meeting of 1868 were thus faced with a situation in which Fuller had taken over the railway company through the back door and managed, with his financial resources, to complete the work they had started. As the railway was now open and achieving the things that Fuller wanted them to achieve, he promptly resigned as chairman of the board, so that the company could vote to pay him back the considerable sum of £12,000 it had cost him to put matters right and finish the railway.

The contractor, Frederick Furniss, was also owed a large amount of money, which was growing still further as he was running the passenger and freight train services on the line, using an aged tank locomotive and some equally old Ex-L&SWR carriages. The shareholders did not have the railway that they had at first envisaged, but instead had a line that actually functioned and operated trains. The overall amounts spent both before and after Frances Fuller took over as Chairman amounted to £82, 275, against which was the original paid up capital of £54,564 with a further £21,300 raised for the projected extension of 1864. This situation produced a debt of £11,321 and a period in the hands of the official receiver, who took over the company in 1869.

The company was about to move into a new era and would be controlled by a small group of men, who ran the railway's affairs until the Southern Railway took over on 1 January 1923. Prominent among these new directors was Thomas Egger, a London Lawyer, who was chairman of the board until the railway grouping. Both Thomas Egger and Philip Rose, a fellow director, acted quickly to get the company back on its feet and out of the hands of the official receiver, by raising new capital to pay off the railway's creditors and the contractor. This quick action resulted in the company becoming solvent by 1872 and out of the official receiver's hands.

The company now faced a situation of having to find or purchase new locomotives and rolling stock to operate the line; this situation would bring extra financial burdens on the company. The solution to this problem came in January 1872, when the London Brighton & South Coast Railway took over all the operating and maintenance of the line, paying the company an annual fixed sum of £2,000, plus £150 for rent.

After a period of unease lasting twelve years, the company now looked forward to quieter times, without the problems of the day to day operation of the railway. Under LB&SCR management, the line started to pay a steady half yearly dividend of 5 per cent on its 8,000 preference shares, with much smaller amounts on its ordinary shares.

Although the LB&SCR operated the line with some small one-off locomotives at first, it soon replaced this odd collection of motive power with the reliable standard Stroudley A1 Terrier 0-6-0 tank locomotives, that were to become the mainstay of the line from the early 1870s. Likewise, the carriage stock also improved with sets of Stroudley four wheeled, short wheelbase carriages, which went with the A1 Terriers.

The services on the branch operated on a regular basis, connecting with main line trains from Havant station to London and Portsmouth. Quite unlike most of the other branches taken over by the LB&SCR from small local companies, the Hayling Island line still remained a small private company until the grouping in 1923, with the LB&SCR having a contract to run the train services on behalf of the local company.

Despite the quieter pace of life the railway now enjoyed, there were some interesting incidents in the line's existence, including a case brought against the railway company in 1874 by the South of England Oyster Company over fishing rights, which had an interesting outcome when the judge awarded partly in favour of both companies.

The Hayling Railway Company also backed a Bill in 1874, to give the LB&SCR more powers, which was unsuccessful in its passage through Parliament. This was followed up in 1882, with a further Bill by the LB&SCR to take control of the Hayling Island and the Woodside & South Croydon companies. This second attempt was also unsuccessful, in that the Hayling Island Railway remained independent.

Other minor changes came in the form of the change of name from Langstone to Langston, without the E, in 1875 and the renaming of the station at South Hayling, to Hayling Island in June 1892.

The LB&SCR were gradually improving the line during 1889, replacing the track from original bridge rail for new flat bottom rail and in turn replacing the rail again in 1899, with chaired bullhead key way track.

A major improvement came in the period, from 1897-1903, when the station buildings were replaced at Hayling Island, together with the goods shed. The single road locomotive shed at this location was demolished and not replaced, locomotives having to use the joint facility at Fratton shed from then on. The timber viaduct across the channel at Langston harbour was totally renewed at this time also and the swing bridge mechanism overhauled.

In 1911, a number of Stroudley Terriers were rebuilt with Marsh boilers, in order to extend these useful locomotives' lives, becoming class A1X; in this form the Terriers were to see their time out on the Hayling Island branch, lasting in service until November 1963 and becoming some of the oldest locomotives in regular service in Britain.

Unlike other parts of the south coast, nothing much happened or changed on the Hayling Island branch during the First World War, with a regular passenger and freight service on the line throughout the conflict, operating its normal timetable. After the war, the Hayling Island branch again settled into a regular timetable, which during the summer months, became more hectic.

The railway was affected by the 1921 Railway Grouping Act, when the local private company at last became part of a bigger concern, that of the Southern Railway group. On 1 January 1923, the Hayling Island Railway Company ceased to exist and the line became absorbed into the newly formed Southern Railway. There was little change at first, in that the locomotives and rolling stock were painted in LB&SCR livery and the stations and goods shed at Hayling Island were likewise in that company's colours. Later, when time permitted and the need arose, the buildings were repainted into the Southern Railway's colour scheme of buff and green and gradually the locomotives and rolling stock likewise followed in the new Southern Railway livery.

Often the trains on the branch ran as mixed services with an A1X Terrier, a single brake carriage and a string of mixed goods wagons, with a brake van at the rear. During the summer, there was often a two train service, with Terriers operating the trains of up to four carriages, taking holiday makers to Hayling Island and returning them home, after a day out from London. The locals called the branch the Hayling Billy, in recognition of its pleasant antiquated look and the now aged Terriers that operated the service.

There was something very British about this gentle back water, with its lined olive green Victorian tank locomotives and aged panelled carriage stock, running at an easy pace through grassy embankments and across a long timber viaduct to a small brick and tiled terminus by the sea. At each timber-constructed halt, the small A1X Terrier would seemingly pant like an overheated dog, while the Westinghouse brake pump clanked and clattered, building up air for the locomotive's brakes. Like a gypsy train on a magical journey, through an enchanted world, the Terriers wound their steel path, from dawn to dusk, week after week, seemingly without a fuss. The trains and the railway were a part of that world and age often referred to in John Betjeman poems that were so much a part of pre-war England, a lost world of sand in the sandwiches and clotted cream with scones.

At Langston, the road traffic was often held up, waiting for a train from Havant or a service from Hayling Island, which had stopped at the timber halt, to pick up a single passenger. Despite the summer heat and the vexation of having to wait,

the comical sight of the little Terrier, often dwarfed by its carriage stock, crossing that road brought many smiles to bad tempered motorists; such a sight could only happen in an eccentric country like England, where emmet-like trains ran between hedgerows. There was something special and mystical about a train crossing a long timber viaduct in the orange summer evening twilight, or even ghostly about the sight in winter, of a Terrier after dark, with white frothy steam coursing out of its long black chimney, hauling a train of two or three dimly yellow lit, non-corridor carriages, as it fussed its way towards Langston Halt.

To all who witnessed this idyllic pre-war scene, things were seemingly forever, but a world war and post-war austerity were to take their toll and the post-war world, with its hardships and selfishness, would destroy so many good things, including enchanting branch lines, like the Hayling Island line.

During the Second World War, the line continued to serve the local population but the holiday makers and day trippers had gone, as the coast was a restricted war zone. From September 1939 to May 1945, the line ran its regular time table, with no extra summer services, as the tourists were not allowed to be there, unlike the military who often used the line to reach their place of duty.

After the end of hostilities in Europe in May 1945, the branch slowly returned to its pre-war self, with a revised summer timetable for the short 1945 season. In 1946, things had improved, with a more frequent train service approaching the years before the war and holiday makers returning to their old summer haunts. Things were to a large extent back to normal by 1947, the final year of the Southern Railway before the network was nationalised. On 1 January 1948, the railways in Britain became nationalised and the newly formed Southern Region of British Railways was now responsible for the Hayling Island branch.

It would take a while for the new administration to put its stamp on the network, with main line operations feeling the first effects of any outward change, branch lines like the Hayling line being far down the list of priorities. Gradually, over the next two or three years, the line began to see the first vestiges of change, with locomotives and rolling stock starting to receive their new liveries and rolling stock appearing in a repainted state, with their new numbers.

By the early 1950s, the Hayling Island branch had taken on a new corporate look, with the Terrier tank locomotives in lined black and sets of green and sometimes carmine red painted carriage stock, while freight stock now sported either a grey or bauxite livery, depending on whether it was fitted or non-fitted. The Terrier tanks were now showing their age and clearly thought had to be given to a future replacement for these venerable antique Victorian survivors.

In 1955, British Railways published its modernisation plan, which was the death knell for steam traction and the traditional railway; from now on, priority would be given to introducing diesel and electric traction to the national network. Despite the heavy investment in the construction of 999 new standard class steam locomotives since 1951, covering all types needed for current traffic needs, the management of British Railways had decided to replace steam with indecent haste, regardless of economic practicality, or the suitability of the new traction on offer from British Railways' designers or the outside locomotive building industry. Branch lines, like the Hayling Island line, fell between several stools, as the line made a modest profit and served a defined purpose, quite unlike other branch lines across the network, which often made a definite loss and were a burden to the overall system. What was to happen in Britain was quite unlike what was happening in the rest of Europe, where the replacement of steam traction was measured and gradual, over a period of two and a half decades.

The Hayling Island branch was clearly a candidate for dieselisation or electrification, as it connected with two main lines from London to Portsmouth and should have been marked down for future modernisation and retention. Attempts were made to improve the motive power issue in the late-1950s, when an Ex-SE&CR P class 0-6-0 tank locomotive, number 31325, was trialled on the branch during May 1957, in an attempt to see if this would solve the future needs for more modern motive power. The eight Wainwright, Robert Surtees-designed small 0-6-0 tanks, which were thirty years younger than the William Stroudley-designed Brighton Terriers, should have fitted the bill, but unfortunately, after trials on the branch with a member of the class, they were found lacking and unsuitable for this role.

The next move should have been to examine the possibility of using the Hampshire diesel units on the branch, which were being introduced from 1957 on branches and cross-country lines in Hampshire and parts of Sussex. The timber viaduct at Langston probably precluded their use for weight reasons; however, a new road bridge was constructed in the late 1950s, which could have been adapted to allow the branch to cross on a separate deck constructed next to the road on a new rail alignment, from the Langston end of the line. This new arrangement would not have cost a great deal, using modern methods of bridge design and construction. Like so many other opportunities of a similar nature, British Railways missed the chance to improve and enhance a part of the network that could and should have survived into the present day.

Unfortunately, there were those in the organisation who had hidden agendas and vested interests who were playing politics behind the scenes. Ernest Marples, the Minister for Transport in the Conservative government in the late 1950s and early 1960s, was one of those people with such a vested interest, being a joint partner in a road building company,

Marples Ridgeway. It was Ernest Marples who hired Richard Beeching in 1961, from outside the industry, to produce the report, *The Reshaping of British Railways*, which led to so many branch and cross country lines being closed. The way that the survey was carried out meant that the figures for lines like the Hayling Island branch were often deliberately incorrectly recorded by the survey team, to justify closure. It's also very interesting that a lot of the key documents justifying such closures from the survey in the early 1960s are missing from the public records, giving a one-sided story.

At the time of the general election in 1964, when the Labour party won a slim majority, Harold Wilson, the Prime Minister, promised to reinvestigate the proposed closures and after the election victory, decided not to rescind what Beeching had advocated. After the 1959 election, when the Conservatives returned to power, it was decided to break up the British Transport Commission, which acted as a coordinated umbrella body over all the nationalised main public passenger and freight operators. Part of the result of this was a policy of closing loss-making lines, which was set in motion before the Beeching report of 1963. One of the lines listed for pre-Beeching closure was the Hayling Island branch, which was originally due to close in 1962. As a result of opposition to closure by local people in the Hayling and Havant area, pursued through the local Transport Users' Consultative Committee, it was decided to give the branch a stay of execution, until alternative improved bus services were introduced.

It was decided to monitor the branch and the improved replacement bus service, over a six-month period, to evaluate if the new road replacement bus operations were adequate and feasible to solve the transport needs of the Island after the branch closed. As a result of this monitoring period, it was decided that buses could replace the rail service on the branch and a date was set for closure on 4 November 1963. The final day of regular passenger operation was Saturday, 2 November, when a normal timetabled operation ran until 2.20 pm, after which a special last day service operated, for all those who had travelled from far and wide to sample the delights of this Victorian oddity.

A1X Terriers, numbers 32650, 32662 and 32670, operated the train service during the last day, while in the evening, all the remaining freight stock was cleared from the line, on the 7.54 service, which ran as a mixed train. The very last passenger operation, the 8.39 pm from Havant, being operated by A1X Terrier 32662, left twenty minutes late and after arrival at Hayling Island, returned at 9.00 pm, with a six carriage formation, headed by A1X Terrier 32650, with 32662 at the rear. At each of the intermediate stations, there were crowds of locals to say goodbye to their local service, which had served the island for almost a century. As the last train progressed along the branch and at each halt, detonators were set off and crowds sang *Auld Lang Syne*, resulting in the final service not arriving at Havant until 9.50 pm Passengers had to make haste across the platform and footbridge at Havant, to catch the last fast train to London, which had been held for them that night, but for the Hayling Island branch, it was all over bar the shouting.

The following day, Sunday, 3 November, a very last special operated over the branch, with A1X Terriers 32636 and 32670, toping and tailing the train. This last train, organised by the Locomotive Club of Great Britain, traversed the line in the afternoon, using the two oldest surviving Terriers as its motive power. There was an attempt to set up a preservation project, in the aftermath of the line's closure, using a second-hand former Blackpool single decker tram, however this was a still born project and came to nothing. Today, you can walk most of the line's formation, from Havant to Hayling Island, where only the old goods shed remains, in use as a local meeting hall.

Train Services

At the time of the Hayling Island line's opening there were five trains in each direction, each day, however this frequency changed over the decades, allowing for extra services in the summer months. For several years, the train service increased to fourteen trains in each direction during the day, Monday to Friday, operating throughout the year, with one extra service in July and August. All the services called at all intermediate halts, except the 6.30 am from Havant, which did not call at North Hayling. Other services did not call at North Hayling, during the timetables for the winter 1959-1960, together with some mid-day and evening services; this practice was discontinued in the 1961 timetable.

Saturday services in the winter months consisted of fifteen trains, operated at hourly intervals, but between the peak summer period from June to September twenty four trains were run in each direction. Between the hours of 9.45 am through to 6.49 pm, a half hourly train service was operated, stopping trains taking 13 minutes and fast nonstop services taking 10 minutes.

Sunday train services only operated between mid-April and mid-September. Until the commencement of the peak summer service in June, an hourly service was operated, with train departures from Havant 10.35 am through to 7.35 pm. During the summer peak period, a service was operated of twenty trains, departing Havant 10.05 am through to 8.05 pm.

There was no separate timetable for freight services, allowance in the timetable for mixed train operation to take place, this normally being operated on the 6.30 am from Havant, 2.58 pm from Hayling Island; these trains operated Monday to Friday, with an allowance of an extra five minutes in the timetable for their operation.

Locomotives and Rolling Stock

Locomotives in the Furniss contractor's period

The Hayling Island Branch is primarily associated with the Stroudley Terrier class 0-6-0 tank locomotives, which operated the train services on the branch for most of the line's existence. However, in the early days there were other locomotives used on the branch, starting with an 0-4-2 saddle tank locomotive, number 1, of unknown origin, which was used during the construction of the line and for a time after the introduction of the passenger service. This machine had 3ft 6inch driving wheels, 11x18 cylinders and a haycock firebox, supplied by Isaac Watt Bolton, of Ashton Under Lyne, the famous supplier of second and third hand locomotives to contractors and minor railways.

Locomotive number 2 was also supplied by the same company, being originally an outside cylinder 0-4-0 tank, constructed by George England, of Hatcham Iron Works, Old Kent Road, later reconstructed as an 0-4-2 tank. This machine had a set of trailing wheels that were larger than its driving wheels, the main drivers being 2ft 10in in diameter and the trailing wheels being 3ft in diameter and cylinders of 9½x13. Both locomotives were later sold back to Isaac Watt Bolton, in 1871.

A third locomotive was acquired by Furniss around this time to replace the first two machines, this being a 2-4-0 saddle tank, named *Wotton*, which also came from Isaac Watt Bolton. This was originally a tender locomotive, which had been converted to a saddle tank by Isaac Watt Bolton at his yard in Ashton under Lyne; this last locomotive was later, after the LB&SCR takeover, returned to its supplier.

LB&SCR Locomotives

The Hayling Island branch had an eclectic selection of locomotives, during the early period of LB&SCR operation, the first being a Sharp, Stewart 2-4-0 Tank locomotive number 96, constructed in 1869, which had a bell mouth safety valve casting and a domeless boiler and weighing 18 tons, 8 cwt. This locomotive had originally operated on the Kensington shuttle service from London Bridge, as part of the London suburban network. Number 96 was later reconstructed, with a full cab, improved sanding gear and enlarged water tanks, which increased capacity from 300 to 410 gallons, which increased the locomotive's weight to 19 tons 8 cwt. In its reconstructed condition, number 96 ran on the Kemp Town branch in Brighton before transfer to Fratton, to work the Hayling Island line.

During its life time, this locomotive had several names and numbers, carrying the name *Kemp Town* until June 1874, after which it became number 115 Hayling Island and was again renumbered 359 in June 1877, being yet again given a new number in January 1886, when it became 499. It left the Hayling Island branch in 1889; it had been put through Brighton works and given a new boiler in 1888, being further reconstructed in 1890, when it emerged from works as number 481, a 2-4-2 Tank, named *Inspector*, with a modified rear end, incorporating a passenger compartment for inspecting engineers, finally being withdrawn in 1898.

A second Sharp, Stewart 2-4-0 Tank, numbered 53, was purchased in 1873. This locomotive, later named *Bishopstone*, also ran on the Kensington shuttle service, before being transferred to Newhaven, where it worked on the harbour contract, from 1875-1878. Number 53 was later renamed *Fratton* and renumbered 270 in 1878, when it was transferred to work on the Hayling Island branch. Number 270, *Fratton*, was withdrawn and sold to George Cohen & Son scrap dealers for £164 in 1890.

The next locomotive to be used on the branch was a Kitson product, number 76, named *Bodmin*, which had been purchased by the LB&SCR in 1869.This machine was originally an 0-4-0ST, which was reconstructed as an 0-4-2ST and named *Bognor*, when it was used on the Bognor branch. This locomotive was in its life time renumbered twice, becoming 358 and later 496. Later, a further Kitson-constructed machine operated on the branch, this being a 2-4-0 Tank locomotive number 248 later renumbered 463, named *Hove*.

Stroudley Terriers
The best-known locomotives to operate on the Hayling Island branch were the Brighton works-constructed Terrier tanks, or Rooters, introduced in 1872 and designed by William Stroudley, who was Locomotive Carriage and Wagon Superintendent of the LB&SCR from 1870-1889. Stroudley was responsible for modernising the LB&SCR locomotive department and standardising the locomotive fleet, which under his predecessor John Chester Craven had developed into a messy affair, with a fleet of odd locomotives, often one and two off designs, constructed whenever a new branch or main line was opened.

The Brighton Terriers, or A1 Class, were his first standard locomotive for the LB&SCR, allowing older worn out machines to be withdrawn or reconstructed into more useful locomotives. There were fifty Brighton Terriers constructed between 1872-80 in batches, mostly being used originally for London suburban work on the South London line, from London Bridge to Victoria and the East London Railway, from New Cross to Shoreditch and Liverpool Street. The class was later to be found on other lines across the LB&SCR system including the Hayling Island branch. The first members of the class were withdrawn in 1901; however, it was quickly found that these by then old but reliable locomotives were of interest to other operators, especially newly opened light railways and some main line companies, who were willing to purchase examples.

In 1911, D. Earl Marsh, the then Locomotive Carriage and Wagon Superintendent of the LB&SCR, decided to reconstruct and reboiler a number of the surviving A1 class, the modified version of the locomotives becoming A1X Class, the X standing for Reconstructed. One of the lines where the A1X Terriers made their home was the Hayling Island line, where members of the class could always be found. Members of this small but powerful class operated the trains on the branch from the late 1880s to the closure of the line in November 1963.

An attempt was made by British Railways in the mid-1950s to replace the Terriers with Ex-SE&CR P Class 0-6-0 Tanks, but after experiments with a member of the class on the Hayling Island branch, it was decided that although they were by then eighty years old, the Stroudley Terriers were superior in every way to the much younger Surtees-designed, Wainwright 0-6-0 Tanks.

Carriage Stock

The original carriage stock used on the line comprised of a number of old Ex-L&SWR four wheeled vehicles, supplied by Fairbank, the line's contractor, together with the line's early locomotives. These four wheeled carriages were withdrawn when the company arranged for the LB&SCR to operate the line. The LB&SCR provided a fleet of carriage stock, mostly Craven, Stroudley and later Billinton four and six wheeler stock, in the nineteenth and early twentieth centuries, which were later replaced as early bogie stock became available.

By the first decade of the twentieth century, the branch briefly had a period of motor train operation, with Marsh and Billinton pull push stock and motor fitted Terriers. Later, Billinton non-corridor bogie stock was used, supplemented by non-passenger-carrying bogie and six wheel luggage vans for parcels and perishable traffic, also for the extra amount of luggage during the summer season.

After the formation of the Southern Railway in 1923, vehicles from the other constituents started to arrive on the line, including Ex-L&SWR non-corridor bogie stock and later steel bodied Maunsell corridor carriages.

During the British Railways era, the line had a variety of carriage stock, including Ex-LB&SCR and L&SWR bogie non-corridor stock and from the late 1950s Maunsell and Bullied bogie corridor vehicles.

In the last five years of the line's existence, BR Mk1 non-corridor suburban carriages were used, including the fibreglass-bodied experimental carriage, sometimes referred to as the plastic coach, which is now preserved at Cranmore, on the East Somerset Railway.

Freight Services

The Hayling Island branch was the last line in Britain to operate mixed trains, which ran on a regular basis in the daily timetable. The mainstay of the freight traffic was coal, which was delivered to Hayling Island station almost until the end of traffic in November 1963.

The branch also had a limited amount of general van and merchandise traffic through most of its existence; this petered out from the late 1950s onwards.

Isle of Wight Wagon Ferry
There had been a railway wagon ferry, from the Langston Harbour to Bembridge on the Isle of Wight.

The vessel used was the *Carrier*, launched in Greenock in 1858 and originally used as one of the ferries on the Firth of Tay service, which linked the railways North and South of the river. The ferries had been part of a project instigated by Sir Thomas Bouch, who designed the first Tay Bridge, which unfortunately collapsed shortly after it opened in 1879.

Carrier was made redundant in 1883, after the second Tay Bridge was constructed and opened, after which it was sold to the Isle of Wight Marine Transit Company, who operated it on a freight ferry service.

The company got into financial trouble in 1886, after which the LB&SCR took over for a time and tried to turn things around. However, this did not happen and the service was withdrawn in 1888.

Hayling Island Transport Proposals
There were several tramway schemes proposed from the late nineteenth and early twentieth centuries, one scheme that was put forward in 1900 involving a tramway from Hayling Island station along the southern coast of the island to Eastoke. This project was promoted by Thomas Pollock and Joseph Phillits of Manchester. Also, in April 1903, a project was proposed to construct a conveyor bridge between Portsmouth and Hayling Island; neither of these schemes were carried out.

London Brighton & South Coast Railway Period

Hayling Island Station, then called South Hayling, shortly after the LB&SCR takeover of train services c.1872, with a train consisting of Sharp, Stewart 2-4-0 Tank *Hayling Island* and a rake of early four wheeler carriage stock. The platform is crowded with railwaymen and local worthies, including the station master, in his top hat. *(Author's Collection)*

Sharp, Stewart 2-4-0 Tank *Bishopstone*, here seen at Newhaven, during the harbour contract: note the dumb buffers, for contractors' use.
This locomotive ran on the Hayling Island branch in the early LB&SCR period of management.

Sharp, Stewart 2-4-0 Tank *Hayling Island* had a very eventful life, being constructed for the LB&SCR in 1869, initially numbered 96, whilst working on the Kensington Branch in London. After being fitted with a cab and being named *Kemp Town*, the locomotive was operated on the branch of that name, until 1874, when it was re named *Hayling Island* and re numbered 115, for use on the Hayling Island branch.

The little Sharp, Stewart ran services on the branch for fifteen years, being shedded at the single road shed at Hayling and Portsmouth. In 1877, it was again re numbered 359 and was yet again re numbered in 1886, as 499, before being rebuilt, with trailing wheels, into a 2-4-2 Tank inspection locomotive in 1889, being named *Inspector* and numbered 481. In this form, 481 *Inspector* was withdrawn in 1898 and broken up. *(Author's Collection)*

Locomotive 496 *Bognor* was constructed by Kitson's in 1868, being purchased by the LB&SCR for £1,140 and was originally numbered 76. The locomotive operated on branches, across the LB&SCR in its early life, before arriving on the Hayling Island branch in 1889, where it worked until 1891.

It was during its time on the Hayling Island branch that it received its new number 496, before departing for Eastbourne, where it worked local train services, being withdrawn in April 1895. *(Author's Collection)*

Stroudley Terrier number 663 *Preston* heads a train of four wheeled stock near Langston c. 1908; these handsome 0-6-0 Tanks were the mainstay of the train services on the branch from the 1880s until closure in November 1963. *(O.J. Morris/Author's Collection)*

A second view of a Stroudley Terrier near Langston, this time number 78 *Knowle*, on a service to Hayling Island c. 1905, again hauling a rake of four wheeled stock, with a Stroudley full brake parcels vehicle. *(O.J. Morris/Author's Collection)*

Hayling Island station c. 1900, with a train in the platform headed by a Stroudley Terrier and a rake of seven four wheeled carriages. The Terriers were very powerful for their size, being quite able to haul heavy long trains of carriage stock and were often seen on main line duties, hauling heavy bogie stock, while performing pilot turns at main line stations like London Bridge or Victoria. *(Author's Collection)*

HAYLING ISLAND RAILWAY STATION 1610

Hayling Island Station c. 1912, with a train running into the station from Havant. This is a good view of the station buildings when the structure had a full awning and also shows the platform arrangement to good effect; note the period adverts and gas lamps.

(Commercial Post Card/Author's Collection)

A1X Terrier 655, formerly *Stepney*, runs around at Havant c. 1920. From 1901, some members of the Terrier class were withdrawn for scrap; however, it was quickly found that there were ready customers who would be willing to purchase these useful powerful small locomotives. The then locomotive superintendent, D. Earl Marsh, realised these locomotives were still of great use to the company and authorised the reconstruction of a given number of them from 1911. The reconstruction entailed a new boiler and extended smoke box, which gave the locomotives a longer boiler barrel and smokebox overhang. The Terriers reconstructed in this form did not lose their good looks, still having a certain Victorian, Edwardian charm about them. *(R.C. Stumpf Collection)*

The Isle of Wight Wagon Ferry

The Wagon Jetty at Langston, after the ferry service to the Isle of Wight had ended c. 1888. The service worked from this jetty at Langston to Bembridge on the Isle of Wight. The wagon ferry was operated by the Isle of Wight Marine Transit Company, from 1884-5, when the company ran into financial difficulties, after which the LB&SCR took over the company and tried to make the service pay. There were problems with the second-hand ferry vessel, named the *Carrier*, as it had a flat bottom and did not perform well on the Solent in rough weather, originally being constructed for the more sheltered Tay estuary, where she had originally worked, before the first Tay Bridge was constructed. The vessel had spent some time working on the Firth of Forth, after its time on the Tay. *(Author's Collection)*

The only known photograph of the *Carrier*, here seen in 1882 at Burntisland, before its commencement of operations from Langston to the Isle of Wight. *Carrier* was repaired at Newhaven Harbour in 1882 before being sent to Langston to operate the wagon ferry service, being withdrawn in 1888 and sold by the LB&SCR. *(Southern Railway official)*

The Southern Railway Period

A1X Terrier number B662 at Havant station after arriving with a train from Hayling Island c. 1925. Both the locomotive and the Ex-L&SWR arc roof Panter bogie brake carriage are newly painted in the first rendering of Maunsell dark olive green. *(Author's Collection)*

On another day, B662 simmers and waits, at the head of its train of former L&SWR Panter arc roof bogie non-corridor carriages, at Havant station c. 1926. The A1X Terrier still has condensing pipes and Westinghouse brake pump fitted, in this mid-1920s picture. *(Author's Collection)*

A view of the far end of Havant Station, showing the stock blocks at the end of the bay platform and the goods yard. The pair of Ex-LC&DR six wheel carriages are of interest as are the warehouses behind the far sidings. *(Author's Collection)*

A1X Terrier 2653 stands at the head of its train of mixed former LB&SCR and L&SWR non-corridor bogie carriage stock c. 1932. By this time, the B had been replaced by a two at the head of the number, hence the 2653; This picture shows the complicated track layout at Havant to good effect, with the angled cross over in the yard, forming part of the locomotive turn out. *(Author's Collection)*

A rather grubby Terrier, number 2661, simmers in the bay platform with a train of Ex-LB&SCR arc roof Billinton stock, as Southern Schools class 4-4-0 tender locomotive number 928 *Stowe* rolls into the main line platform with a service from London Waterloo to Portsmouth Harbour c. 1935. The young boy in a white shirt seems to be propping himself up against the Terrier's cab, while talking to the locomotive's crew. *(S.W. Baker)*

A while later, after running around its train of two Billinton carriages, the same Terrier and the same boy continue their conversation in the afternoon sunshine, c. 1935. This is a good view of the station and goods yard, showing the ware houses and the interesting track layout.
(S.W. Baker)

On another occasion, 20 September 1936, Terrier 2655 simmers in the bay, awaiting the road to Hayling Island, while a group of passengers talk and walk up the platform. *(Author's Collection)*

Running across the run around loop, Terrier 2662 runs into the sidings to make ready for its next turn of duty c. 1935. This is a good photograph of an A1X Terrier painted in the later lined, Maunsell light olive green livery. *(Dr Ian C. Allan)*

A1X Terrier 2661 heads an excursion train of non-corridor stock out of the up bay platform at Havant station c. 1933. This train will have to traverse the main line to reach the Hayling Island branch on the south side of the station. *(Author's Collection)*

A1X Terrier 2661 waits in the bay at Havant for the road to Langston and Hayling Island c. 1937, while the train guard chats to the driver. Note the station reconstruction taking place and, in the background, an electric set is entering the station, bound for Brighton or London Waterloo. *(Author's Collection)*

A1X Terrier 2662 heads out of Havant, through the cutting towards Langston, with a single Panter Ex-L&SWR bogie carriage, on its way to Hayling Island c. 1930. *(M.D. England)*

Terrier 2655 hauls a mixed train towards Havant on 30 August 1949, which includes an Ex-LSWR Surrey Warner bogie corridor brake vehicle and a long line of freight stock, including vans and open coal wagons. *(C.M. & J.M. Bentley)*

A1X Terrier 2644 heads a service bound for Havant consisting of two Panter non-corridor brake vehicles c. 1938. *(Author's Collection)*

The approach to Langstone station, with Terrier 2635, heading a train of two Ex-L&SWR Panter brake carriages, on a Hayling Island service, c.1938. *(Author's Collection)*

A family in a Model T Ford wait at the level crossing at Langston for a Terrier to pass with a service to Hayling Island, which has an Ex-LB&SCR Billinton bogie brake carriage leading, c.1930. *(Author's Collection)*

Portrait of a masterpiece. A1X Terrier number B662 stands at Langston station, with a train of Billinton carriage stock c.1926. This picture in so many ways sums up the British branch line, with a small tank locomotive blowing off, at the head of a set of vintage carriages, on a warm summer's day. *(O.J. Morris)*

A mixed train near Langston Harbour, headed by A1X Terrier 2655, made up of a two car set of Ex-L&SWR Panter, non-corridor bogie stock and a string of interesting open wagons, consisting of private owner coal wagons and examples from the other big four railway companies. *(OJ. Morris)*

Across the timber viaduct to Hayling Island, Terrier 2662 coasts, with its mixed train of Ex-LB&SCR and L&SWR bogie non-corridor stock c.1936. *(Author's Collection)*

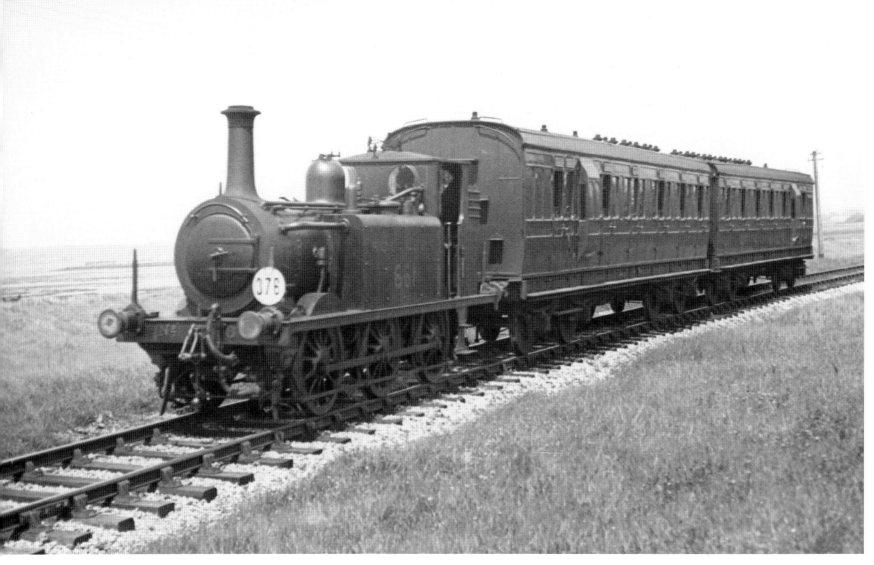

Terrier B661 heads a train of Panter Ex-L&SWR non-corridor bogie brake vehicles between North Hayling and Hayling Island c.1926.

(Dr Ian C. Allan)

A1X Terrier 2678 heads a train of mixed carriage stock, near Hayling Island on 29 May 1939. Note that this locomotive has a Drummond chimney; by this time some members of the class, especially those on the Isle of Wight, were acquiring some Ex-L&SWR fittings.

(L.C.G.B. Ken Nunn Collection)

A1X Terrier 2644 running with the same mixed set of carriages, on 29 May 1939, between North Hayling and Hayling Island station. *(L.C.G.B. Ken Nunn Collection)*

British Railways Days

A1X Terrier 32640 waits at the head of a train of pre-grouping bogie stock at Havant c.1951. 32640, formally number 40 *Brighton*, had spent many years on the Isle of Wight after being purchased from the LB&SCR by the Isle of Wight Central Railway in January 1902, becoming their number 11, reconstructed as an A1X in July 1918. In 1923 it became Southern Railway W11, being named *Newport* in October 1928. W11 retained its lined Maunsell livery through the Second World War, before being returned to the mainland in February 1947, where it was overhauled at Eastleigh works, renumbered 2640 and painted unlined black, before going on loan to the K&ESR. 2640 was overhauled, renumbered 32640 and repainted in BR lined black in March 1951, before being despatched to Newhaven. 32640 spent many years on the Hayling Island branch, being withdrawn from Brighton shed in September 1963, after which it was purchased by Butlin's for display at Pwllheli holiday camp and is now preserved at the Isle of Wight Steam Railway. *(Author's Collection)*

32640 brings the 2.20 train from Hayling Island into the bay platform at Havant on 2 June 1956, while 32650 waits in the siding to back onto the 2.35 back to Hayling Island. *(R.C. Riley)*

On 10 August 1963, 32650, in its later lined BR black livery, waits in the bay at Havant with its train for Hayling Island. The Terrier sizzles in the damp rainy atmosphere, as a family walk past, the father admiring the little Victorian tank locomotive, as they pass by. *(R.C. Riley)*

32646, formerly LB&SCR 646 *Newington*, waits at the head of its train of mixed bogie carriage stock at Havant station c.1961. 32646 had a very varied history, in that this locomotive had been purchased by the L&SWR in March 1903 along with sister locomotive 668 *Clapham*, for use on the Lyme Regis branch. The Terriers became L&SWR numbers 734 and 735, working at various locations, after their time at Lyme Regis.

In July 1913, 734 was hired to and later purchased by the Freshwater Yarmouth & Newport Railway, on the Isle of Wight, becoming their number 2, after the grouping in 1923 becoming Southern Railway W2, named *Freshwater* in October 1928 and was reconstructed as an A1X in 1932 and renumbered as number W8.

During the Second World War, number W8 was repainted unlined black, being returned to the mainland in April 1949 and after an overhaul at Eastleigh works, returned to traffic as 32646, in unlined black. 32646 operated on the Hayling Island branch for many years, together with other allocations to Brighton and Newhaven, being finally withdrawn in November 1963 and sold to the Hayling Terrier Fund, for use on the proposed preserved Hayling Island branch. However, as this project did not succeed, it was later sold to Charles Ashby of the Sadler Railcar Company and was moved to Droxford, on the closed Meon Valley line. The locomotive was again sold in May 1966, to Brickwoods Brewery, to stand outside their pub, The Hayling Billy. Later in June 1979, W8 *Freshwater* returned to the Isle of Wight and is now part of the Isle of Wight Steam Railway. *(Dr Ian C. Allan)*

32650, formerly LB&SCR number 50 *Whitechapel*, taken from the run round loop at Havant on 25 July 1959. In 1901, the Terrier became number 650, reconstructed as an A1X in May 1920; after the grouping in 1923, it became Southern Railway B650. 32650 had an interesting working life, as this locomotive also spent time on the Isle of Wight, from May 1930 until May 1936, where it became W9 *Fishbourne*.

After returning to the mainland in May 1936, it was stored at Eastleigh until April 1937 when, after an overhaul, the Terrier became 515S and was sent to Lancing carriage works. 515S was converted to oil firing in August 1946, which was not a success, being quickly reconverted back to coal firing. In August 1953, 515S was overhauled and transferred to capital stock, as 32650, for use on the Hayling Island branch, which was short of Terriers with the larger Isle of Wight coal bunker.

The locomotive became a regular on train services, on the branch until the end of services, hauling the last public train on 2 November 1963. 32650 was sold to Sutton Borough Council for preservation, as a replacement for 32661, the real *Sutton*, which was cut up by mistake at Eastleigh in 1964. Originally preserved on the K&ESR, it now resides on the Spa Valley Railway in Tunbridge Wells. *(J.H. Aston)*

A rear bunker end view of 32670, formally LB&SCR number 70 *Poplar* and later Kent & East Sussex Railway number 3 *Bodiam*, here seen at Havant station c.1960. This Terrier also had an eventful life, in that it was sold by the LB&SCR in 1901, to the Rother Valley Railway, later K&ESR, becoming their number 3, being reconstructed to A1X in 1943.

The design of coal bunker is of interest, in that it was constructed at Rolvenden on the K&ESR, when the locomotive was reconstructed in the mid-1930s, from parts obtained from several Terriers, including number 71 *Wapping*, which had become K&ESR number 5 *Rolvenden*. The Ex-Great Western 0-6-0 saddle tank, K & E S R number 8 *Hesperus*, had a similar bunker fitted at Rolvenden also. Number 3 became B R number 32670 in 1948 and was overhauled and repainted from K&ESR apple green, to unlined black in 1950. 32670 operated at different times over the Hayling Island branch from 1954 to 1963, after which it was purchased and preserved by the Wheel Brothers, of Brighton, who kept the locomotive on the Kent & East Sussex Railway. It is now owned by the Terrier Trust. *(R.C. Riley)*

32640 again at Havant, on 4 August 1962, with a train of modern Bulleid and Maunsell steel bodied bogie stock, which by the 1960s had gravitated to the branch from main line duties. *(J.H. Aston)*

Interlude at Havant, with A1X Terriers 32670 on a train bound for Hayling Island and 32662, waiting in the loop for its next turn of duty, c.1962. *(R.C. Riley)*

32640, with an unusual carriage formation, heading a train of Southern Bulleid stock and a single Ex-LMS vehicle at the head of the train, on 25 July 1959. *(J.H. Aston)*

32640 waits in an empty platform to depart Havant with a train for Langston and Hayling Island, the two carriage train consisting of a single Maunsell brake and a BR-constructed Mk1 suburban ALL SECOND c. 1962. *(Bruce Oliver)*

32640 takes water at the far end of Havant station on 6 April 1956, a study of the large size of the L&SWR water crane and the miniature Victorian tank locomotive. *(Graham T.V. Stacey)*

32661 also takes water in this mid-1950s picture taken at Havant, which shows the signs for passengers wishing to go to the local Warner's holiday camp. *(Author's Collection)*

In the last years of the branch, number 32650 is being filled up for another run to Hayling Island, surrounded by ash and the untidy paraphernalia of this watering point, at the end of the station. *(R.C. Riley)*

On 18 August 1963, 32670 hauls a train of mixed steel bodied stock on an empty stock working from Fratton to Havant, for use on the branch, here seen arriving in the main line up road at Havant station. *(R.C. Riley)*

32677 departs Havant with a train for Hayling Island c.1955 and is about to pass through the level crossing, before running south to Langston station. 32677 was a frequent locomotive on the line in the 1950s, after being returned in 1949 from the Isle of Wight, where it had been W3, later after 1932, W13 *Carisbrooke*. 32677 was withdrawn in October 1959 and cut up at Eastleigh. *(Online Transport Archive)*

32677 again on the same day, at the same location, with the same formation of carriage stock, including an additional Ex-L&SWR bogie non-corridor brake vehicle. The carriages at the rear of the train are painted in gulf red, while the Maunsell brake vehicle is painted Southern Region malachite green. *(Online Transport Archive)*

32677 runs bunker first towards the approach to Havant station, with a train from Langston. This picture shows the level crossing and the water tank, at the eastern end of the station. *(Online Transport Archive)*

Taken from a train window, looking forward towards the locomotive, this is the approach to Havant, viewed from the south, as the train passes the outer home signal bracket, nears the curve, taking the line across the level crossing and into the station. *(Online Transport Archive)*

32650 hauls a single Ex-L&SWR Panter bogie carriage, through the cutting between Havant and Langston on 12 March 1955. *(E. Gamblin)*

32678 heading a three carriage formation of steel bodied stock, made up of two BR-constructed Mk1 non-corridor suburban vehicles and a single Southern Railway, Maunsell corridor brake end, in August 1962. This photograph was taken from the brick bridge featured in the previous picture. *(P.H. Groom)*

At an earlier time, 28 July 1956, 32650 heads a train of panelled Ex-L&SWR Panter stock and a single B R steel bodied suburban carriage along the cutting. *(J.H. Aston)*

32662 heads a four carriage train of Ex-L&SWR Panter bogie, non-corridor stock, near Langston c. 1955; at this point, the line ran through woods and farm land, before arriving at the level crossing and station at Langston. *(Author's Collection)*

32640 arrives at Langston platform, with a service for Hayling Island c. 1960. The Terrier has interesting features acquired during its eventful lifetime, including a Drummond chimney, tool box and enlarged IoW coal bunker and a spark arrestor, fitted in BR days. *(T. Wright)*

The station at Langston, looking towards Havant, showing the concrete platform and basic station buildings, with their clapboard construction. The building had a waiting room/booking office and an office, which doubled up as a booking clerk's office for selling tickets, c. 1962.

(Rail Archive Stephenson)

Langston in the mid-1950s, showing the platform, constructed of parts supplied by the Southern's Exmouth concrete works and the timber station building. This station was reconstructed to this configuration in the 1930s, when a number of upgrades were authorised during the Southern Railway period. There was a siding serving a wharf that ran off from a location near here and a second siding, which was constructed after the Second World War, leading to a loading platform. *(Online Transport Archive)*

32650 simmers in the cold November air, steam drifting across the adjacent allotments from the small Victorian Terrier locomotive. This is the last public day of operations, 2 November 1963, and the last time motorists will be held up at the crossing to allow this antiquated gipsy train to make its way to Havant or Hayling Island. *(R.C. Riley)*

The ground frame at Langston station, on 2 November 1963, with staff in attendance for the last day. *(R.C. Riley)*

32662 nears Langston from the timber viaduct, with a train made up of a converted Maunsell brake vehicle, now a pull and push driving trailer and the BR MK1 suburban plastic carriage, which utilised the underframe of a carriage damaged in the Lewisham railway disaster in 1957, here seen on 18 August 1963. The plastic carriage is now preserved on the East Somerset Railway at Cranmore. *(R.C. Riley)*

32662 belching black smoke, heading the 2.54pm train from Hayling Island, has just crossed the timber viaduct with a long mixed train, on 25 August 1950. This picture shows the amount of freight traffic that still existed on this branch in the immediate post-war period. This traffic dwindled in the mid to late 1950s, until only coal and a small amount of van traffic existed, at the time of closure in November 1963. *(G.F. Bloxam)*

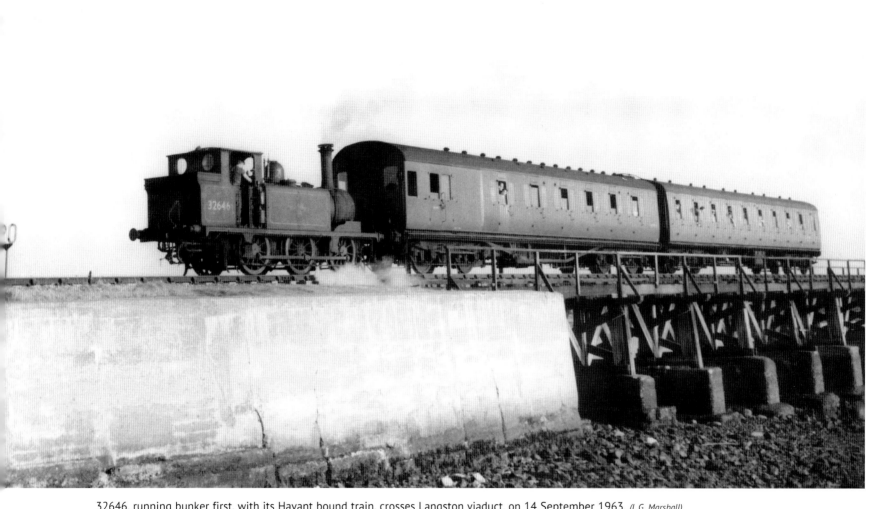

32646, running bunker first, with its Havant bound train, crosses Langston viaduct, on 14 September 1963. *(L.G. Marshall)*

On a cold wet winter afternoon, 32650 hurries its Hayling Island bound train towards the swing bridge, in the centre of Langston viaduct. This was 2 November 1963, the final day of public services; tomorrow a special would run the length of the branch for the last time, bringing down the curtain on almost a century of train services, on the Hayling Island branch. *(R.C. Riley)*

A Victorian period picture of the swing bridge in use, showing the centre span open, allowing shipping to pass through. After the Second World War, the bridge was seldom opened for shipping and although the swing bridge was maintained in full working order, it was rarely opened after the early 1950s. *(Author's Collection)*

In this mid-1950s picture, 32650 heads a train of Ex-L&SWR non-corridor stock, across the timber viaduct. This picture shows the construction and design of the viaduct to good effect, detailing the decking and stanchions which, in Southern Railway days, were strengthened and set in concrete, to prevent rotting to the lower timbers. *(Author's Collection)*

32678 heads a train of Maunsell and Bulleid carriage stock towards North Hayling, on 4 August 1962. This illustration shows in detail the complicated timber construction of this structure, which was a contributory factor in the line's closure. The need for renewals and the cost of maintenance almost guaranteed the line's eventual demise. Note the new road bridge in the distance, which could have been designed with a separate rail deck, to allow trains to cross on one side. *(J.H. Aston)*

In the evening twilight, a Terrier runs bunker first across Langston viaduct, with a service to Havant c. 1963. *(Online Transport Archive)*

A beach level view of the viaduct showing the timber construction of the structure and the signal box, controlling the swing bridge, taken from the North Hayling side. *(Online Transport Archive)*

North Hayling was a bleak station, in a bleak landscape; here we see a train calling at the station in the final summer of services in 1963.
(Online Transport Archive)

A general view of the station at North Hayling, showing the clapboard-constructed waiting room and the long open timber platform, with only a rough wooden seat for comfort, in the summer of 1963. In pre-grouping days, there was a siding near this location, with a platform to load oysters from the adjacent oyster farm that existed at that time. *(Online Transport Archive)*

Ex-Kent & East Sussex Railway number 3 *Bodiam*, 32670, stands at North Hayling platform, with a train for Hayling Island in the summer of 1963, a long way from the Rother Valley and the Kentish Weald. *(Bruce Oliver)*

A Terrier and train skirt the shore on their way to Hayling Island station; this picture shows the openness of this part of the island, with its wild windy landscape, twixt land and sea. *(Online Transport Archive)*

A grubby 32646 runs along the section between Hayling Island station and North Hayling, with a train for Havant in the summer sunshine of 1963. *(Bruce Oliver)*

A Terrier makes its way along the bleak open coastal section, with its two carriage train, bound for Hayling Island in the summer of 1963.
(Online Transport Archive)

A burnished 32677 heads its two carriage train along the coast line towards Hayling Island station in the winter of 1957. This former Isle of Wight locomotive would be withdrawn in 1959; note the LB&SCR copper capped chimney. *(Pamlin Prints)*

An interesting train movement, with two Terriers, running top and tail, with a three carriage formation, seen between Hayling Island and North Hayling stations c. 1957. This was a way of moving a locomotive from one part of the branch to another without having to create a special light engine movement and also allowing such a movement across the Langstone viaduct which had a weight restriction. *(H.F. Wheeler)*

32678 makes light smoke along the coastal section, on 4 August 1962, before going inland for the final part of the journey to Hayling Island terminus. *(J.H. Aston)*

A going away picture of a train bound for Hayling Island, summer c.1963. *(Online Transport Archive)*

A newly returned and overhauled 32677 approaches Hayling Island terminus, with a train of Ex-L&SWR non-corridor carriage stock, from Havant in September 1949. The A1X Terrier is largely still in Isle of Wight condition, including its post-war, lined malachite green livery, applied at Ryde works, when it was number W13 *Carisbrooke*. The Terrier has the full British Railways, in Bulleid sunshine lettering, and still sports an LB&SCR copper-capped chimney. *(C.C.B. Herbert)*

32646 approaches Hayling Island terminus in this 1962 picture, hauling its load of two bogie carriages, a Maunsell brake and a BR Mk1 suburban composite. Note the interesting array of Southern Railway rail built upper quadrant home signals, controlling the outer reaches of the approach to the station. *(Online Transport Archive)*

32650 arrives at Hayling Island, with a single Ex-L&SWR brake vehicle c. 1955; this is an interesting picture, featuring an LB&SCR lower quadrant, wooden posted outer home signal. *(Author's Collection)*

A head on picture of Terrier 32646 at the head of the approach and goods yard, of Hayling Island station c. 1955; note the line side permanent way hut on the right. *(Author's Collection)*

An interesting panoramic view of Hayling Island terminus station, c. 1960, showing the track layout, the station and goods yard. This view also shows the buildings to good effect and the position of signals controlling the whole inner complex. *(R.K. Blencowe Collection)*

32646 shunts in the goods yard c. 1962, note the front splashers sand boxes; these were a feature retained from its reconstruction during its time on the Isle of Wight, members of the class reconstructed on the mainland having under running plate sanding equipment and round forward splashers, the only exception to this being Kent & East Sussex Railway number 3 *Bodiam*, later 32670, which was reconstructed as an A1X at St Leonards depot near Hastings in 1943, using a spare boiler, from the Southern Railway, retaining its front splashers, with the original sand boxes. *(Online Transport Archive)*

On the same day, 32646 couples up to a set of mixed BR and Southern Maunsell stock in the goods yard, while preparing to depart with a service to Havant c. 1962. This is a good overall view of the station and track layout; also featured is the locomotive coal stage, which normally had an open wagon full of coal, on the adjacent siding. *(Online Transport Archive)*

On 8 May 1950, 32646 runs into the goods yard while shunting. This locomotive is painted in plain post-war unlined black, with Bulleid sunshine lettering, in the first BR style of livery, applied in 1948. Note the concrete posted loading gauge, another product of Exmouth concrete works, and the ground shunt signal in the middle background. *(Author's Collection)*

An interesting photograph of the north end of Hayling Island station, showing the ground frame signal cabin centre and the storage building on the far left, as 32640 runs light into the bay platform. This is a good picture of the two LB&SCR lower quadrant wooden posted home signals, which controlled departing trains at this location, seen here on 6 April 1956. *(Graham T.V. Stacey)*

Another picture of the northern end of Hayling Island station, this time in c. 1955, with 32677 in the main platform, next to the original LB&SCR running in board, this was later removed and replaced. *(Online Transport Archive)*

32650 simmers in the platform awaiting departure with a train for Havant, c.1956, painted in its earlier lined black livery, with the smaller numbering and early BR emblem. This picture also shows the original running in board and the goods yard on the far left, including the other side of the loading gauge. *(R.C. Stumpf Collection)*

Five years later in 1961, by now the LB&SCR running in board has gone and been replaced by a series of benches on the platform, also a flower bed has been added in the foreground. 32646, in its later B R lined black livery, now sports the later 1956 BR emblem and the carriage stock has been upgraded to modern steel bodied carriages. *(R.C. Stumpf Collection)*

Any chance of a cab ride; an enthusiastic member of the public looks as if he has struck lucky and cadged a lift to Havant on a Terrier. This interesting picture shows the station buildings and awning, at platform level, looking south towards the buffer stops, summer 1963. *(Bruce Oliver)*

Our old friend 32677 at the end of its journey from Havant, with a train of mixed steel and wooden panelled carriage stock c. 1955. This picture shows the station buildings at this time, with the cut back awning and the main building now bereft of any cover from the elements.
(Online Transport Archive)

Holiday makers pour off the train as 32662 stands in the platform with a plume of black smoke drifting vertically above its chimney. This illustration, taken on 18 August 1963, shows how much holiday traffic was still using the line, only three months before closure. *(R.C. Riley)*

32661, in a dusty condition, stands in the main platform, after arriving with a service from Havant on 25 July 1959. The Terrier has a gaunt look about it, standing at the head of a train comprising two Bulleid bogie corridor carriages and a single BR Mk1 suburban vehicle, bringing up the rear. *(I.H. Aston)*

Above and overleaf: A sequence of three pictures, showing 32650 arriving with a train and running around the loop, before going over to the coaling stage to be replenished with fuel, in preparation for working the next service back to Havant, all taken on 2 November 1963, the last day of public services.

This locomotive operated services on the branch for much of the post-war era and after withdrawal in 1963 was purchased by Sutton Borough Council, to be a centrepiece in their new civic centre. Originally number 50 *Whitechapel*, it was renamed *Sutton*, as a replacement for the real *Sutton* 32661, which had been cut up by accident at Eastleigh, after withdrawal in 1963. However, fate decreed otherwise and 32650 was instead first loaned to the Kent & East Sussex Railway and is now on the Spa Valley Railway, in Tunbridge Wells. *(R.C. Riley)*

32650 was also used on the final day of services, 2 November 1963, to haul the final freight train from Hayling Island to Havant, here recorded about to depart on that day from Hayling goods yard. *(R.C. Riley)*

In May 1957, Ex-SE&CR P class 0-6-0 Tank number 31325 was trialled on the Hayling Island branch, here seen around that period; note the raised bunker rails and the larger buffers. The P Tank was not a success on the branch and was quickly returned to more humble duties elsewhere. *(E. Gamblin)*

A Selection of Signalling

An interesting example of a Southern Railway-constructed bracket home signal, controlling the approach to Havant from Langston, with rail built supports and Ex-L&SWR lattice signal posts, supporting steel upper quadrant arms, outside Havant 5 May 1950. Note also the single aspect colour light signal KW69 and shunt signal, lower centre, and the single home signal in the background controlling the line to Langston, from Havant far left. *(Author's Collection)*

An unusual arrangement of two upper quadrant Southern Railway steel distant arms, attached to a former LB&SCR wooden post, here seen on 5 May 1950, between Havant and the woods near Langston station. *(Author's Collection)*

A fine example of a former LB&SCR wooden posted bracket home signal, here seen on the outer approach to Hayling Island station, 5 May 1950. Note the former LB&SCR wooden posted, single home signals in the background, which control the line from the platforms at Hayling Island to North Hayling station. *(Author's Collection)*

The same bracket signal from behind, showing the mechanism and counter weights. *(Author's Collection)*

The Main Line through Havant

Havant station c. 1905, with an L&SWR, London bound passenger service, headed by a Drummond T9 4-4-0 and an Adams T1 0-4-4 Tank locomotive shunting in the goods yard. This station was originally constructed by the LB&SCR as part of its route from London and the coast line from Brighton to Portsmouth, however, in 1858 a second main line arrived in Havant, that being the Portsmouth Direct line, which had been a speculative venture by contractor Thomas Brassy, who eventually sold the new railway to the L&SWR, who promptly fell out with the LB&SCR over running rights to Portsmouth. After Parliamentary intervention, the line became a joint operation, allowing both companies to run trains from Havant to Portsmouth. This is a good picture showing the complicated track arrangement running into the Hayling Island bay platform and the equally complicated signalling. *(Commercial Post Card)*

The same scene c. 1920, with an LB&SCR passenger train arriving, on a coastal or London bound service. The track work is still complicated, with slips and sharp curves in the goods yards and Hayling Island bay platform, also the signalling is still very nineteenth century, with the LB&SCR home signals on long wooden posts, looking towards Portsmouth. *(O.J. Morris)*

An LB&SCR Billinton B2 4-4-0 heads a passenger service for Portsmouth, towards Havant station c. 1910. This view shows the junction between the LB&SCR on the right and the L&SWR Portsmouth direct line, on the left. The signalling for both junctions is LB&SCR home type on long wooden posts, controlled by the box at the eastern end of Havant station. *(O.J. Morris)*

Fratton Locomotive Shed

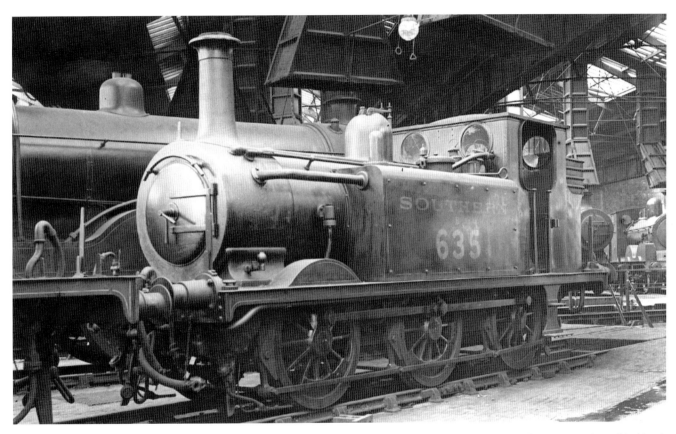

Fratton Depot supplied the motive power for the Hayling Island branch, for most of the line's existence. The Terriers mostly resided in the round house, that once existed there, which in pre-grouping and later in Southern Railway days had an allocation of both LB&SCR and L&SWR locomotives. Here we see A1X Terrier B635, on one of the storage roads, awaiting its next turn of duty, painted in the early Maunsell dark olive lined green livery c. 1925. This locomotive is of interest, in that it has a number of features, including a flush riveted smoke box; it still has its condensing pipes and has been fitted with enclosed coal bunker rails. *(Author's Collection)*

2659 in later condition, with its new number, allocated after the letter prefix was dropped, for each of the former constituent companies. This A1X Terrier is painted in the later, Maunsell light olive green, has a riveted smoke box, still retains its condenser pipes and, like B635, has enclosed coal bunker rails, on 25 June 1939. *(Author's Collection)*

2659 in later condition, painted in war time austerity unlined black, with Bulleid sunshine lettering. The locomotive has had its condenser pipes removed but still retains its Westinghouse brake pump, c. 1947. *(J.H. Aston)*

Also in war time unlined black, A1X Terrier 2661 with Bulleid sunshine lettering, stands in the round house at Fratton, awaiting its next turn of duty; note the circular riveted patch on the smoke box, where the condenser pipe was once located, c. 1947. *(J.H. Aston)*

The Hayling Island Branch in Colour

Only a week before closure, 32650 simmers in the bay at Havant station, with a train for Hayling Island, while children and a handful of enthusiasts wait to take a last trip along the line. *(Bruce Oliver)*

Terrier 32678 waits in the siding at Havant, as 32640 arrives with a train from Hayling Island, on 17 June 1962. *(Nick Lera)*

32640 leaves Havant, with a service for Langston and Hayling Island, in the summer of 1958, the Terrier hauling an interesting formation of a new BR Mk1 surburban carriage in Gulf Red livery and a Bulleid 1st class corridor vehicle. *(Online Transport Archive)*

32650 emerges from the brick over bridge between Havant and the cutting leading to Langston station, on 26 October 1963, while heading for Hayling Island. *(Bruce Oliver)*

In the summer of 1963, 32636 heads a train of BR Mk1 suburban and a Maunsell brake vehicle, through the trees towards Havant. This picture shows how small the A1X Terriers were, with the fireman having to stand outside the cab to have a comfortable ride on the footplate. *(Nick Lera)*

The same fireman looks out of the cab of 32650 running bunker first with a three carriage set of BR and Maunsell stock, 21 July 1962, near Langston. *(Bruce Oliver)*

On 17 June 1962, 32678 heads bunker first out of Langston towards Havant, with a train of Maunsell carriage stock. *(Nick Lera)*

Ex-K&ESR number 3 *Bodiam*, B R 32670, arrives at Langston station with a train from Havant in the summer of 1958, while the porter signalman operates the levers of the ground frame. *(Online Transport Archive)*

32662 arrives at the same location on 21 July 1963, heading a train of BR Mk1 suburbans and Maunsell carriage stock. *(Bruce Oliver)*

On 17 June 1962, 32640 coasts into the platform at Langston, with a train of Maunsell corridor stock, note the original Ex-LB&SCR station running in board, still in situ until closure. *(Nick Lera)*

32646, running bunker first, runs between Langston viaduct and the station on 29 July 1963, hauling a mixed train, containing a single former LMS standard van and BR Mk1 suburban carriage stock. *(Bruce Oliver)*

32650, hauling an unusual formation of a pull and push driver trailer and a BR Mk1 all second carriage, leaves the viaduct at Langston in this autumn scene in October 1963. *(Online Transport Archive)*

32661 crosses the viaduct with a service for North Hayling and Hayling Island, on 17 June 1962; this is an interesting rake of Maunsell corridor stock, including a 2nd class open vehicle, next to the locomotive. *(Nick Lera)*

A mixed train of corridor and non-corridor vehicles, crosses the viaduct headed by 32650, heading for North Hayling station, on 21 July 1963.
(Bruce Oliver)

In the late afternoon winter sunlight 32650 and a two carriage train, made up of a BR Mk1 surburban all 2nd and a pull and push driving trailer, crosses Langston viaduct, the sun glinting across the locomotive and train, as it makes its way to North Hayling, while boats stand peacefully in the harbour, October 1963. *(Online Transport Archive)*

Twilight of the Terriers; a dusk scene taken near the same location, with a Terrier and the same train formation, on 26 October 1963.
(Bruce Oliver)

32650 heads its Havant-bound train towards Langston Viaduct, in the autumn of 1963, only months before the line's closure.

(Online Transport Archive)

32670, running bunker first, heads its train towards Langston viaduct, with a service for Havant from Hayling Island on 7 July 1963. The concrete blocks along the shore line are sea defences to try to stop the erosion along the beach at this point. *(Bruce Oliver)*

32661 arrives at North Hayling station in the summer of 1958 with a service to Hayling Island, consisting of three Maunsell corridor carriages. The three passengers on the platform slowly make ready to board the train, for the short journey to the line's terminus. *(Online Transport Archive)*

On 17 June 1963, 32640 eases into North Hayling station platform with another service for Hayling Island. The train formation is of interest, being made up of a four carriage train of Maunsell and Bulleid corridor stock, showing how intense the train service could be in summer, on this coastal branch line. *(Nick Lera)*

A view taken from near the sea shore of 32662, with a mixed three carriage train on 21 July 1963 as the Terrier slows to pick up passengers, at the timber platform at North Hayling. This is a good picture of the platform and the basic waiting accommodation provided, more like a lineside hut, than a station building. *(Bruce Oliver)*

32650 near North Hayling with a train of mixed carriage stock in the summer of 1963; the Terrier has burnt the paint off its smoke box in this picture. The train sweeps around the curve, showing a stretch of water, leading to Langston Harbour, in the background. *(Online Transport Archive)*

Steam envelopes the train as 32650, running bunker first, heads for North Hayling, with a train for Havant, on 26 October 1963. As the autumn turns to winter, closure beckons for this semi-rural, seaside branch line; who will provide the service next summer? *(Bruce Oliver)*

On the same day, 32670 also heads bunker first, at the same location, with a train of mixed passenger carriage stock. *(Bruce Oliver)*

32661 makes a fine sight, as it sedately heads its two carriage train of bogie stock towards Hayling Island on 7 August 1962. The Terrier's smoke box is scorched along its left hand side and the spark arrestor has taken on a drunken angle, in this picture. *(Bruce Oliver)*

On 21 July 1963, 32650 heads a train of Maunsell and a solitary BR Mk1 surburban carriage, towards Hayling Island. Despite the dirty condition of the smoke box, the staff at Fratton have found time to clean the sides of the bunker and side tanks of the little Terrier. *(Bruce Oliver)*

In the summer of 1963, 32640 runs bunker first between Hayling Island and North Hayling, with a train of mixed Maunsell and Bulleid corridor stock for Havant. *(Nick Lera)*

On 7 June 1962, 32640 heads out of Hayling Island with a service for Havant, consisting of two BR Mk1 suburban carriages and a single Maunsell corridor brake vehicle. 32640 still has much of the features and fittings it acquired on the Isle of Wight; note the tool box on top of the side tank and the enlarged coal bunker, fitted during its time hauling trains on the various branch lines on the Island. *(Nick Lera)*

The same set of carriage stock, with 32678 in charge, running along the stretch of line between Hayling Island and Hayling North, in the summer of 1963. 32678 also spent time on the Isle of Wight, having the same enlarged coal bunker, but having small leading splashers, without a sand box, sanding being applied from below the footplate on this locomotive. *(Nick Lera)*

32661 steams hard for Hayling Island terminus, in this picture taken on 17 June 1962, hauling the mixed carriage set described earlier.

(Nick Lera)

Arriving at Hayling Island in the summer of 1958, 32650 enters the outer limits of the station with a train of Maunsell corridor stock from Havant. Note the Southern Railway rail built bracket signal and the Exmouth works concrete fence posts. *(Online Transport Archive)*

A grubby 32670 arrives at Hayling Island terminus, on 21 July 1963, with the Maunsell pull and push driving trailer leading the formation. 32670 had a Stroudley copper-capped chimney, when taken into BR stock in 1948; this was exchanged for a Marsh, cast iron chimney in 1960, when 32655 was sold to the Bluebell Railway, the latter locomotive receiving the more original Stroudley chimney. *(Bruce Oliver)*

A panoramic view of Hayling Island station platform, on 26 October 1963, with a train of BR Mk1 suburban carriages and a Maunsell brake vehicle standing in the platform with a Terrier waiting for the signal to depart. With less than a month to go before closure there are many passengers, taking a last ride for posterity. Note the BR 20 ton brake van in the siding; there was still a bit of freight until the end of services, three weeks later. *(Bruce Oliver)*

Where Terriers meet; 32678 arrives with a train from Havant, while 32661 waits in the bay with the return working on 7 June 1962. Hayling Island station had many interesting operating features, including lower and upper quadrant home signals, which were controlled by a ground frame, here seen at the end of the platform. The line was worked by staff and ticket and here we see the porter signalman about to receive the token from the driver of the incoming train. *(Nick Lera)*

A general view of Hayling Island terminus, on 7 June 1962, with 32661 waiting in the bay for the incoming train to arrive. The platform is neat and tidy, with a line of seats along its length, leading to the station overall canopy and main buildings. *(Nick Lera)*

A group of boys look on as 32650 is about to be coaled for its return trip to Havant on 26 October 1963, only a week before it would haul the last train on the line. Note the substantial goods shed in the background and the generous size of the goods yard, with its track work radiating out. *(Bruce Oliver)*

A disinterested member of the station staff walks past recently arrived 32650 with its train of two carriages, on 26 October 1963. Soon, the fast frequent service to Havant would be no more and almost a century of train services on the island would come to an end. *(Bruce Oliver)*

A relatively clean 32650 eases forward to run around its train, while a woman muses by the fence, looking on at the spectacle. The line still has a reasonable number of passengers at this late stage in its existence as children and adults file through the ticket barrier on their way to the sea on 26 October 1963. *(Bruce Oliver)*

The Last days

32662 arrives at Hayling Island terminus, with a train on the final day of public operations, 2 November 1963. The locomotive is decorated with a floral tribute and the trains that day were full of enthusiasts and members of the public, taking a last ride on The Hayling Billy.
(Bruce Oliver)

On the following day, the Locomotive Club of Great Britain ran the very last train, the Hayling Farewell Rail Tour, which traversed the line for the final time. The Hayling Island part of the tour was handled by the two oldest Terriers, 32636 and 32670, the former K&ESR locomotive, number 3, Ex-LB&SCR number 70 *Poplar*. Here we see Ex-Newhaven Harbour Company, Ex-LB&SCR number 72 *Fenchurch* heading the train to Hayling Island on 3 November 1963. *(Online Transport Archive)*

Both the Terriers returned the LCGB tour double headed to Havant and here we see them both at the Terminal bay platform after the return trip; both are now preserved, 32636 on the Bluebell Railway and 32670 on the Kent & East Sussex Railway. *(Bruce Oliver)*

Fratton Depot

32636 receives a repair at Fratton Depot in June 1963, five months before the end of her service with British Railways. This locomotive had a lucky escape, as it was involved in a rear end collision which might have resulted in the locomotive being withdrawn, had it not been for the senior works foreman at Eastleigh having the locomotive repaired, knowing the Bluebell Railway wanted to purchase it for preservation. *(Bruce Oliver)*

Newington, The Hayling Billy Pub Sign. After the line had closed and been demolished, in the late 1960s, Brickwoods Brewery set up a theme pub on Hayling Island, which was called the Hayling Billy. A fund had been set up to preserve a Terrier, for the unsuccessful attempt to preserve the branch, which resulted in 32646 being preserved. 32646, having no preserved branch to work on, went to the Vector Rail project, based on the Meon Valley railway in Hampshire. After this project finished in the late 1960s, 32646 was sold to Brickwoods Brewery, to become a pub sign; later, after the brewery was taken over, the locomotive was donated to the Isle of Wight Steam Railway, where it is now preserved as Freshwater Yarmouth & Newport Railway number 2, Southern Railway W8 *Freshwater*, as seen outside the Hayling Billy Pub on 7 August 1968. *(Bruce Oliver)*

The outside pub sign at the Hayling Billy Pub, 7 August 1968. *(Bruce Oliver)*

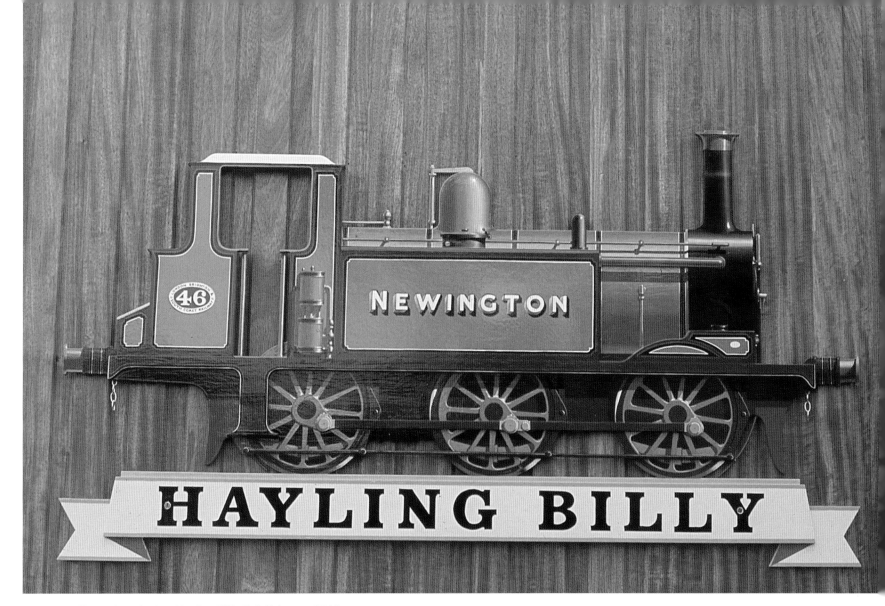

The main pub sign, Hayling Billy Pub 7 August 1968. *(Bruce Oliver)*

Appendix

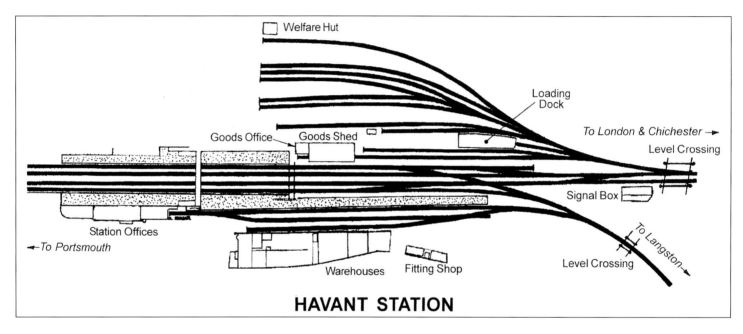

HAVANT STATION

Welfare Hut

Loading
Dock

To London & Chichester →

Level Crossing

Goods Office   Goods Shed

Signal Box

Station Offices

To Langston →

←To Portsmouth

Level Crossing

Warehouses   Fitting Shop

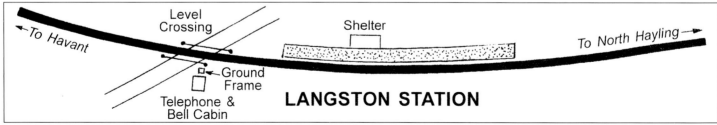

LANGSTON STATION

←To Havant

Level
Crossing

Shelter

To North Hayling →

Ground
Frame

Telephone &
Bell Cabin

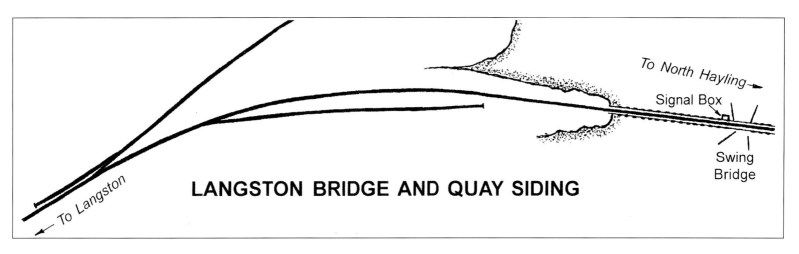

LANGSTON BRIDGE AND QUAY SIDING

To North Hayling →

Signal Box

Swing Bridge

← To Langston

Shelter

NORTH HAYLING STATION

← To Langston

To Hayling Island →

Site of oyster track and platford

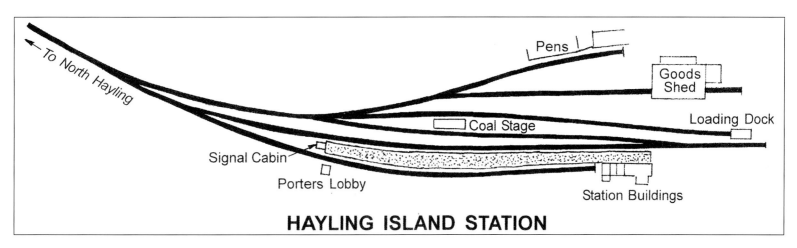

To North Hayling

Pens

Goods Shed

Loading Dock

Coal Stage

Signal Cabin

Porters Lobby

Station Buildings

HAYLING ISLAND STATION

Acknowledgements

I would like to thank the following people, for their kind help during the compiling and writing of this book:
Peter Harding, for producing the map and track plans and his kind advice and help whilst writing this work; Peter Waller, of the Online Transport Archive, for black and white and colour material; Nick Lera, for allowing me to use his colour pictures from the 1960s; Bruce Oliver, for the use of his black and white and colour pictures; and Richard Stumpf, for the use of numerous pictures from his extensive collection.

I would also like to mention some sadly now deceased railway photographers, including R.C. Riley, H.F. Wheeler and S.W. Baker.

Also, Vic Mitchell, Keith Smith and Alan Bell, who wrote *Branch Line to Hayling* published in 1984, and in addition, R.G. Harman, who wrote *The Hayling Island Railway* published in 1964.

The following books were also used for reference: *William Stroudley*, H.J. Campbell Cornwell, David & Charles 1968; *The Brighton Terriers*, C.J. Binnie, Ravensbourne Press 1969; and *The Island Terriers*, M.J.E. Reed, Kingfisher Railway Books, 1989.

(I have tried to contact all copyright holders of pictures used in this book, however, if I have missed anyone out, please contact the publishers.)